Shattered Greatness
"The Beauty Of Salvation"

Table Of Content

FOREWORD

I have always viewed my life as difficult! I have experienced so my trauma, hardship, and pain, so being shattered became normal to me.

I was raised in a dysfunctional home as a child, without my mother and father, so my childhood started shattered. I was broken because I didn't understand why my mother chose drugs over her children, and my father was married and living his life with his other children.

I was looking for love as a result of childhood abandonment, so as a teenager, I began to make foolish decisions. By the age of sixteen, I was a teen mother, and this caused me to become more shattered than I was before.

I was lost, broken, rejected, and criticized by family members during my pregnancy. I felt alone, misunderstood, and I thought my life was over.

Although I was raised in the church, I had no idea who God really was and that he wanted to make me whole. I also didn't know that no matter how shattered I was, I was still great, and there was a great work for me to do in the kingdom of God.

By the time I was a young adult, I had lost a child. I was forced to bury my baby girl and had no time to mourn. This was the most painful thing that I have ever experienced in my life.

While running from this pain and the shame of being so broken, I met a young man and became his wife within the first six months of our relationship. He was my numbing medicine, but I choose to call it love.

He was clearly not the man for me, yet I continued to chase him, trying to hold on to what I knew was not real. I was shattered, and for some reason, I thought this broken man could put me back together again.

We were completely lost! I was attending church yet rejecting real transformation in God. I was unaware of my greatness because I was way too shattered to see anything good coming out of me.

I was baptized as a child, and I also gave my life to Christ at a young age, but I didn't have a relationship with God. After surviving a very toxic and humiliating divorce, I started a new relationship that I was again, not ready for at all.

I gave birth to three more children out of wedlock, and this pushed me further away from where I desired to be in God. I realized that relationships and sex were a deadly cycle that I continued to go in circles with, and I was tired.

This relationship drained the life out of me, and I almost lost my life because of it. Death was almost my portion.

I was cheated on, lied to, manipulated, and deceived! Heartbreak is not a great word to describe what I went through in this relationship.

I lost my job, became homeless, and had to live out of my car with my children. I was humiliated as a woman and a mother, and he was no help to me at all.

I actually left the church to attempt to get my life back on track, but I did not leave God. I wanted to disconnect from everything that was separating me from Him.

I was desperate to run back into the arms of God to hide and be restored. I wanted every broken piece of me to be at his feet.

I decided to give my life to Christ again, but this time, I understood the beauty of salvation. I was aware of God's love for me and how much he loved me, shattered and all.

As I began to attend church again and rebuild my relationship with God, he began to reveal how much greatness I was carrying on the inside of me. In spite of all I had experienced, God revealed why he allowed me to survive.

Salvation was my portion, so I didn't have to live a defeated life. I was shattered, but I still had a purpose.

When you give God your life, you are exchanging what you do not want to carry any more for the promises that God has already declared over your life. The enemy loves for our brokenness to appear to be the end of us; however, God desires to use every place that we have been shattered to bring him glory.

This book is such an excellent read for those who do not understand the beauty of salvation. It is completely transparent, inspiring, and motivating.

This book is a tremendous blessing to the body of Christ. It is the help that many people need to discover the beauty of salvation.

It reveals how God can take our ashes and give us beauty.

-Pastor Berneka Alleyne

DEDICATION

This book is dedicated to my heavenly father and to everyone who has helped me on my journey to freedom. It was your love, prayers, and encouragement that helped me stay free from the things that were trying to kill me.

There were many times when I almost gave up, but your love lifted me. My pain almost became the death of me, but your love gave me life.

Special thank you to my Pastors, Kevin & Berneka Alleyne, who are also my spiritual parents as well. You have no idea how much I love you both, and I don't know where I would be right now if God had not sent you both to be a part of my life.

Thank you for accepting, loving, and nurturing my children and myself the way that you do. We are so grateful to have you both in our lives.

To my beautiful daughter and all of my handsome sons, thank you for loving me unconditionally. We have come a very long way because of our love for each other.

I dedicate this book to you all because no matter how shattered I was, you have all still called me mom! You have been my strength and my push to keep going the many times I wanted to quit life altogether.

I am blessed to be your mother, and I'm excited about what God is getting ready to do in all of your lives. The sky is not the limit when God is in it.

Thank you to all of my church family, friends, and family members who have supported me. I will never forget your love and kindness towards me.

INTRODUCTION

Life has a way of making you feel like you are at a dead end. This is the very place where everything appears to be shattered in your life, and you see no way up.

When you have experienced so much pain in your life, it is not easy to believe that you are great. The truth is, greatness is the furthest thing from your heart and mind.

This book brings awareness to those who do not know how great they are because of all of the pain they have seen and experienced. I was once this person, but then I became one with salvation.

When I decided to give God my life and completely trust him, he began to show me how the pieces of me that were shattered were still great, and that he was going to bring each piece together to make me whole. I had no idea that my broken pieces still had value, but salvation led me into my greater.

It was salvation that gave me permission to be everything that God has created me to be. I gained the courage to start living past what others thought about me and what I have gone through in my life.

I am a child of God, and not only do I carry greatness, but I also have access to greatness. My shattered pieces were important to God, and so are yours.

This book will help you understand who you are, how to gain wisdom, patience, and faith in God. It will also help you understand the power of salvation.

You may feel like you are in a shattered place in your life right now, or feel like you are broken in many pieces, but this is not the end of you. You were created to be great! Please allow this book to shift you from shattered failure into shattered greatness.

You have the power to overcome everything that you have had to face in your life. I wrote this book to help you.

Salvation has given you the keys to unlock your greatness; I want to help you learn how to use them.

"In the midst of pain, we begin to understand the price Jesus paid for our salvation."
-Cindee Snider Re

CHAPTER 1

"Shattered Salvation"

Salvation is the saving of the soul from sin and its consequences. It is the reason why Christ died for humanity.

When someone receives salvation, they are simply giving God permission to take full control over their lives. It is the process of choosing God's will over our own.

I received salvation when I was about 22 years old. I have been on my journey as a Christian faithfully now since November 2015.

I decided to accept Jesus Christ as my Lord and savior because I wanted more out of my life. I knew that there was more to me, but I was also aware that I wouldn't find it outside of God.

Before receiving salvation, my life was completely shattered. I was battling the spirit of rejection, tied into sin, and I was on the verge of losing my mind.

I was tired of going through the same toxic cycles in my life and doing the things that I knew were not of God. I started to realize that I was way too concerned about what others felt about me.

I was living a lesbian lifestyle, bitter, and confused about many things about my life. I believed salvation would heal, restore, and save me from myself.

I thought when I gave my life to Christ, I would be delivered instantly, and all of my worries would disappear. I didn't know that salvation was the first step towards a new life in Christ, but there was a process when it comes to my deliverance.

I really thought that everything would get better very fast, but it seemed to have gotten worse. I was being talked about, mistreated, and abandoned because of my decision to live right before God, and I was totally shocked.

I saw visions of me being free! I saw my life changed, and my mind renewed, but I did not see the process of receiving all of these things.

I viewed salvation as a fairytale, yet it was not a fairytale at all. It was a huge step, but it was definitely not the last step.

Before salvation, I was shattered. After receiving salvation, I was still shattered.

What I expected God to do once I received salvation did not happen. My perception of salvation was not clear at all, and I had no real understanding of it.

Once I realized that my life did not change overnight, I began to label my season as shattered salvation. This means his grace saved me, but I still needed to allow him to clean me up.

My brokenness was just right for God. I was shattered, but I was still worth everything to him.

I thought my broken pieces were going to be the death of me, but they were really the best parts of me. Broken pieces still work, especially when God is the potter.

The enemy began to attack me more when I received salvation because he wanted to contaminate my perception of who God was in my life. He wanted me to see my brokenness as a death trap and not a route to an abundant life.

I thank God for giving me the courage and the wisdom to see the beauty in salvation. Giving God my life did not guarantee me an overnight success story, yet it gave me access to eternal life if I committed to the journey that God has created for me.

You may have received salvation already and is faithful to ministry, but this does not mean that you can avoid your process of change, deliverance, and breakthrough. Salvation is beautiful, even if the process isn't.

You are still great, and you are carrying greatness. There is still a purpose for your life!

Receiving salvation allows you to receive what God has for you on the other side of your pain. It gives you permission to be great.

The enemy wants you to believe that being shattered is your only portion, but do not accept this lie from him. You are more than your broken pieces.

There are plans and promises that are awaiting your arrival. Salvation is your first transportation to get where you are headed!

It is the vehicle that will carry you into your destiny. You do not need to focus on where you are broken; God will take care of your broken pieces

Do not allow the enemy to cause you to see your salvation as a dead-end; let God show you the beauty of salvation. You may be shattered, but you are shattered greatness.

Salvation is the cure for the shattered. It has the power to put you back together again.

It is the first exit for the shattered. You will never be lost again.

It initiates the comforter to be with you always. You don't never have to feel alone.

Salvation is not intimidated by your brokenness. It is working with your broken pieces, for your good.

Nothing can work against you when God is within you. Nothing can stop you when God is leading you.

Your brokenness does not mean that you can't pursue the liberty and purpose for your life. God's will does not stop or end because of brokenness.

He is still God and will continue to work through you right in the midst of your chaos, turmoil, and brokenness. He will lift you out of the darkness and give you your own light.

I encourage you to embrace salvation and let it work for you. Your broken pieces were already paid in full.

You don't owe the enemy anything but a goodbye. Choose freedom and life over brokenness and shame.

Once your mindset changes, everything on the outside will change along with it.
-Steve Maraboli

CHAPTER 2
"Shattered Mindset"

The mind is one of the most powerful attributes of the human body. It stores thought, memories, dreams, desires, and information that is valuable to us.

It also stores the trauma, pain, and fear that we have experienced in our lives that could be detrimental to our growth, success, and self-confidence.

The mind serves as a compass in our lives. How we think or perceive things is usually who we become.

We are specifically instructed to renew our minds in the Bible, so this should be a priority for believers daily. If we do not renew our minds, we end up stuck where we are and remain stagnated.

After I received salvation, I had to work on the way I think. My perception was contaminated by pain, and I desired to see things the way God did.

Before salvation, I thought my life was fine and everything that I wanted to do, I was going to do it. I thought I was already free.

The enemy had my mind shattered, and he was planning to destroy it. He was literally using my mind against me.

My mindset was very toxic! I was not only convincing myself that it was ok to be a lesbian, but I also thought that I had to put everyone before myself to feel accepted and loved.

I did not know that I was valuable and that God would never want me to be treated less than that by others who said they loved me. My mind was shattered!

My thought process was very toxic and unhealthy. At the time, I didn't know that I was supposed to give my mind to Christ so that he can change the way I think and perceive things about others and myself.

I was unaware of how to make healthy decisions for myself because I wanted to make sure others around me approved of them. I held in many of my feelings because I thought they were not important to discuss with anyone.

When your mind is shattered, so is your life. You are unable to be who God has created you to be because the way you think does not lead you to promises; it leads you to sorrow and pain.

What you think about yourself is how others will begin to treat you. I felt worthless, rejected, and as if I was not good enough, so everyone around me started to treat me as such.

When I received salvation, I realized that God had given me an invitation to come closer to him so that he can renew my mind. I understood more than ever that my mind was shattered, but it was still functioning.

Never allow the condition of your mind to cause you to count you out. God still has a plan for your life, and he still desires to renew your mind.

Before salvation, I battled with many negative thoughts. I was also extremely depressed.

I always kept my home dark, and I didn't go around people too much. I would isolate myself until someone needed my help again, and then repeat this cycle over again.

I was so bound mentally that I couldn't think outside of the familiar. What I knew was all I could handle because I didn't know how to think of myself as greater or see myself in a better place in my life.

I was afraid of change as well because mentally, I couldn't handle being judged or rejected any more than I already was. Some days I would say I'm coming out of this, and then other days, I would lie in bed and hate the day that I was born.

The struggle was real! I battled in my mind every single day, and I just wanted to live a normal life.

I cared about everyone around me and would do anything for them, but I had no love for myself. This caused me to be mentally distraught because I could not understand how I could love others so much and still hate myself.

Salvation taught me how much God loved me and what I was worth to him, so things begin to change slowly. It was and has always been a battle in my mind because I didn't feel wanted.

I believe my battle in my mind began when I was about 12 or 13 years old. Everything I did was wrong, according to my mother, and she had no idea how to cater and love me.

Everything surrounding me was dysfunctional, not to mention, she would use me to do things that were beneficial for her. She used her children to satisfy her selfish agendas, and mentally I didn't understand her ways; it didn't make sense to me.

At 16 years old, I gave birth to my first child, and instead of her supporting me and being there for me as a mother should, she called DCF to attempt to have my daughter taken from me. I was in and out of the system myself, so this was the last thing I wanted to happen to my child.

My mother continued to torment me with calling DCF, and I felt myself starting to hate her. Mentally, I could not understand why a mother would do this to their child.

I started to think I was really worth nothing to her and that nobody cared what happened to my baby girl and me. I was drained from going back and forth with my mother about her actions and dealing with caseworker after caseworker.

At one point I started to battle with suicide thoughts. My mind was all over the place.

I wanted to be accepted by my mother and my family, but I never was. Nothing that I did was good enough or it didn't fit their standards.

I wanted to be accepted and loved like I loved so there was a battle in my mind for a long time. I had no support most of my life, so many times I felt like I was in the wilderness alone.

I saw no reason to live. Seemingly my life didn't matter to those who should have valued me the most so there was no point in being alive.

Salvation saved my life! It gave me a new meaning of who I was and who I belonged to.

Giving my life to Christ gave me assurance that if nobody else loved or appreciated me, God did! Salvation became my spiritual life support.

Giving my life to Christ also revealed to me that taking my life would cause my children to be motherless, and I would die without fulfilling the call and purpose over my life.

I was a single parent raising my children, and the way I was treated, I would have never left my children in the hands of those who were not there for me. God opened my eyes, and I became very grateful for my life.

You may be battling suicide thoughts right now, but don't do it! Give your life to Christ and allow him to be the lover of your soul.

Your journey is not over until God says it's over. Keep fighting and seeking after our father and his will for your life.

As I grew closer to God through prayer, the word of God, and fasting, my mind began to change. I was finally started to have my own mind, and I was no longer concerned about what others thought I should or shouldn't do.

My mind shifted from thinking I was worthless to thinking I was more than enough. I did not think I needed to be accepted by anyone anymore.

Receiving salvation is the first step, but afterward, you must embrace a new mind. Your mind may be shattered right now, but it is not the end of you.

God specializes in the renewing of our minds. When you began to apply his word to your life, you will not be able to think the way that you use to.

Seeking God for a renewed mind was the best thing that I could have ever done. He changed my entire mindset, and he can do the same thing for you.

Every negative thought started to diminish in my mind, and I began to take my mind back. I began to think positive and train myself to avoid being negative.

Suicide thoughts had to flee, and depression had to leave. My mind was being renewed, and I was becoming a better person.

Receiving salvation caused me to be put in a posture that required my mind to be changed. I accepted Christ into my life, and in return, he accepted my mind just as it was and began to change it through his word and his love.

The condition of your mind can be the death of you! Don't just receive Christ; take on the mind of Christ.

I wanted to not only belong to Christ; I wanted to be like Christ. In him, my desires began to change, and my mind started to elevate on levels that I was not aware of.

My mind was shattered, but God still had a plan for me. Salvation allowed me to see the beauty of my mind once I submitted it to God.

With words, I could build a world I could live in. I had a very dysfunctional family, and a very hard childhood. So, I made a world out of words. And it was my salvation.
-Mary Oliver

CHAPTER 3
"Shattered Family"

My childhood was completely shattered! I didn't feel wanted or loved by my biological parents, so I grew up looking for this love and acceptance from others.

I didn't know what real love was from my biological mother, and I couldn't tell you a time I heard a happy birthday, or I love you from her. I don't even remember her giving me hugs and kisses growing up at all.

To some people, these things do not matter, but for me, they did. I didn't ask to be here, but since I was, I believed that my parents were responsible for loving, nurturing, and caring for me.

I was in and out of DCF custody, back and forth with my mother, and then eventually, my mother left me with a family member to raise me. This alone was very heartbreaking and challenging as a child.

I remember seeing other children with their parents, and I would become so jealous and angry because I didn't have mines. It was hurtful and humiliating at the same time.

I could not understand why she would leave us! I kept thinking, "what did we do wrong," "what can I do to make her want me," and when is she coming back!"

I am very grateful for the woman who took us in. No matter what happened, she was right there to pick me up and take me in.

I remember a time when my guardian had to work and asked my biological mom to watch us. My mother agreed, but after we were in her care, she dropped us off to somebody else.

Once again, we had no time to bond with her or be loved by her; she left us again. Unfortunately, the person who she left us with, which was a female, touched me inappropriately under my clothes.

I remember crying, asking her to stop, and she told me to hold on, she was going to take her time. She kept telling me that it was not going to hurt, but I continue to cry because it did.

This was our babysitter violating us. Instead of my mother listening to my sister and me, she continued to call us liars.

The babysitter told my mother that I was a whining little girl and that I was lying about what she had done to me. This shattered me into many pieces that would later lead me down many dangerous roads.

I was also being molested by my biological grandmother's husband and was called a liar when I spoke of it. I was never protected.

My guardian took me to be tested to see if I was being touched, and the test came back positive. I had no reason to lie; I was only a child who desired someone to protect me from those who harmed me.

Unfortunately, my biological parents were not around to do this. I had my guardian, but I wanted more.

I wanted my parents in my life, and I always wanted to know why they didn't want me. I started to realize that my family was shattered, and I believed I would fail in life because of this.

My family member who took on the responsibility to raise me did an incredible job. I will always love and appreciate her for her many sacrifices and love towards my children and myself.

She could not provide the latest shoes, clothes, or toys, but she did everything in her will to make sure that I was cared for and provided for. Although she did her best, I never stopped longing for my mother and father's love.

Many times, I felt empty, lonely, and depressed. I became the child who desired to stay in the house while other children wanted to go outside and play.

I'm the oldest child of ten children, and still, I don't know what family feels like. We have always been scattered and raised by other people besides our parents.

There is nothing like a mother's love, so not having it caused me to build many walls. I lacked trust for others, and I still battle with trusting others as an adult.

After I received salvation, I was taught that I had been adopted into a new family. I was assured that I have a new family who was also believers as I was and that I no longer had to feel abandoned or unwanted by those who were related by blood.

Salvation gave me access to the love that my children and I needed from my pastors and church family. For the first time in my life, we felt wanted and loved genuinely.

The beauty of salvation gave me hope again. It caused me never to abandon my children the way that I was, and always to do my best loving and supporting them,

I also found strength in knowing that my guardian didn't have her mother either as a child. Her mother passed away before they could ever build a relationship together.

She would always tell me that she has my back and that she would never stop praying for me. She always believed in me and spoke greatness over my future.

I never stopped praying for my biological mother, and I never will, but I refuse to allow her lack of love for me cause me to live an unhappy, defeated life. Salvation has given me the right to the tree of life, and I choose to live an abundant life.

You may have grown up in a shattered family, but that does not define who you are. Your true identity is only found in God.

If you have received salvation, you have a family that is excited to meet you and welcome you to be a part of their lives. Blood does not make anyone family; God does.

The enemy will try to use the brokenness of your family to keep you bound to heartbreak, agony, and fear, but you must learn how to remind him that God will never leave nor forsake you. There is a power within you that will enable you to be strong and endure the experience of being a part of a shattered family.

I encourage everyone that will read this book to know that you can and will make it no matter how hard it may seem. Keep pushing, pressing, and looking up to God for everything that you believe you didn't gain from your family.

Nothing will happen overnight, but you are never alone. Embracing salvation gives you an entire new family that loves you.

Put your family in God's hands and embrace his everlasting love. He sent his son to die just for you; this proves that he has created you be a part of his royal family, even when your natural family is torn apart.

Once I understood who I was and who I belonged to, the hole in my heart began to close slowly. I still have my moments, but I stay in control of them.

Find the strength to overcome the condition of your family. Open your heart to see the beauty of salvation.

Our life is full of brokenness - broken relationships, broken promises, broken expectations. How can we live with that brokenness without becoming bitter and resentful except by returning again and again to God's faithful presence in our lives.
-Henri Nouwen

CHAPTER 4
"Shattered Relationships"

Before I received salvation, my perception of relationships was being around others, bonding, and building together whether it was real or not. I believed that relationships were healthy, depending on how I viewed and handled it.

I allowed people to come in and out of my life, use me, and mistreat me and still called in love. I figured everyone goes through things in relationships, romantic or not, and the only way to fix it was time and enduring the hard times with each other.

Although this is true to some degree, It is unhealthy when you don't value yourself and do not have a clear understanding of what a healthy relationship is. My heart had been shattered since I was a child by my parents, so I expected nothing less from anyone else.

I settled for less than what I deserved because I had no idea what I deserved. A shattered heart can't make healthy decisions if it has not been put in the hands of God.

I settled because I wanted to be accepted, loved, and appreciated. This is something that I have always wanted, so I did whatever I felt was right to obtain it.

After suffering abuse and cycles of heartbreak from men, I started to build sexual relationships with other women. I was looking for love from anyone willing to give it to me.

I was totally against this kind of lifestyle, but everything wrong seemed to feel so right, and the enemy deceived me tremendously. I was saved, but I had no real understanding of what this meant for me.

I was going to church and still living any kind of way. I didn't know how to deal with my hurt and pain, so in my heart, this was the easy way out.

During some of these relationships, I suffered abuse physically, mentally, and sexually. I knew I deserved better, but at the time, I had no idea that I was even worth better.

The physical abuse consisted of fights and being pushed. The mental abuse was being blamed for what my partner had done to me physically and having to accept that maybe it was my fault.

These particular battles caused me to slip into depression and silent rage. I suffered sexual abuse when I didn't want to be intimate but was forced to engage to keep that person in a relationship with me.

Sometimes, I suffered physical abuse in front of my children. I would put myself in harm's way before I allowed anyone to hurt them, but in some cases, my son would jump into the fights with me.

I would cry and pray to ask God not to let my children get hurt. If anyone got hurt, I was okay if it was me.

I stayed in those relationships because I thought it was love, and love is something I had always wanted. Wherever I felt love, that's where I would go or stay.

I was afraid to stay and to leave. I believed that the people who were in my life needed me, even if they were not there for me the way that I needed them to be.

I knew there were great people in the world that I did not know yet, but I always dealt with the fear of meeting new people that could potentially walk out of my life. Instead of opening up to meet new people, I put a wall up to block them out.

I needed someone to teach me self-value and self-worth. I needed my parent's love and a clear understanding of how to effectively date and build healthy relationships.

Coming into salvation has shown me I didn't have to stay bound. I was looking for love, hope, and affection in the wrong people when all I had to do was call on the name of Jesus.

I did not have to accept abuse of any kind at all. God has shown me my worth, and if I can't be treated like a queen, I don't want the relationship at all.

Since I have become a woman of God, I don't just trust what anyone says anymore, I pray and ask God to show me that person's heart. I also seek God to find out if he sent the person to my life or if my emotions are leading me.

Salvation will reveal your real value! It will show you how much you are worth and inspire you to set standards for yourself.

I am open to love and marriage, but he will have to be after God's own heart. I recently slipped into a relationship that I was emotionally led into, and I got pregnant.

Yes, I was still saved, but I was growing and learning spiritual discernment and how to master self-control. My baby boy is here, and he has changed my life for the better, but this entire fall with his father opened my eyes even more.

I realized that after I received salvation, I needed to become more aware of my flaws and struggles. I needed to be able to recognize my weaknesses and allow God to help me in this area.

When you receive salvation, you do NOT become perfect. You embrace the love and grace of God that will cover and pick you up if or when you fall.

The beauty of salvation is knowing that your shattered pieces can and will be put back together again. My fall caused me great humiliation and brokenness, but salvation reminded me to get back up and try it again!

I did not have to stay bound to pain and embarrassment. I repented before God and got back to my kingdom's work.

I received liberty from toxic relationships, the homosexual lifestyle, and pain when I understood the beauty of salvation. My heart belonged to God when I became a believer, and no one should have permission to destroy it.

After receiving salvation, it is imperative that you learn how to build a relationship with God and yourself before attempting to build one with anyone else. If you do not start with God and yourself, you will only encounter heartbreak and pain.

When I began to build a relationship with God and myself, I started to desire freedom from every relationship that was unhealthy and toxic for me. My eyes start to open, and my self-worth increased.

I lost my desire to be in a relationship with anyone who was not sent in my life from God. When it comes to homosexual relationships, conviction caused me to run for my life.

I didn't want to die in my mess! I had a choice to either get out of this lifestyle or die in it.

Because of my willingness to build a healthy relationship with God and myself, I am open to real love and genuine friendships. Salvation has shown me that my shattered heart was still great.

It doesn't matter what the condition of your heart is right now, or how many failed relationships you have encountered, God can still use it. A shattered heart is not a destroyed heart, and it still has a purpose.

Salvation has shown me what true love is. It has helped me see love from the eyes of God and not my experience.

I encouraged you to take your shattered heart to God and leave it there. Salvation has given you a new start with love, friendships, and happiness, but it all begins within you.

Souls are God's jewels.
-Thomas Traherne

CHAPTER 5
"Shattered Soul"

The soul is defined as the spiritual part of a human being or the inner being. It is a very vital part of every living being.

Your soul is the part of you that consists of your mind, character, thoughts, and feelings. Most times, people can describe what kind of person you are or speak about your character, according to the condition of your soul.

The condition of your soul will always leak out in your life through the way that you make decisions, respond to test and trials, and how you treat others.

Your soul will ultimately reveal your happiness or distress. You have no power to hide the condition of your soul.

Before I received salvation, I didn't know that my soul was shattered. It was broken, disturbed, and I had no rest.

I was dying on the inside! Internally, I was worn and damaged in my soul.

For years, I had allowed so many things to damage my soul. I had no idea how important it was to cleanse my soul from pain, abuse, and neglect.

The condition of my soul caused me to become bitter, angry, frustrated, and restless. There were too many painful memories, traumatizing experiences, and heartbreak lying dormant in my soul.

When I received salvation, I learned that I didn't have to carry these things in my soul anymore. My soul was now in the hands of Jesus Christ, and he was going to heal it.

My soul was shattered, but it was still valuable to God. He gave me permission to lay down what I was carrying in exchange for rest.

I encourage you to take your soul to God and leave it there. You do not have to remain broken on the inside.

There were so many things going on inside of me from my childhood that I need to be free from. No matter how much I went to church or read my bible, my soul was still desperate for healing.

Please do not thinks that salvation is the final step for your life to make a drastic change. There is still some work for you to do to see change manifest in your life, and the restoring of your soul is one of the things you must do.

Every day will be a new day to pursue the righteousness of God. Your soul will need it.

Once I committed my life to Christ and began to acknowledge the condition of my soul, change start to happen within me. I was healed from rejection, pride, molestation, the opinions of others, and loneliness.

Because of the beauty of salvation, my soul is shattered, but it is free. I am free from the heaviness I use to feel, and I am happy about who I am becoming.

A shattered soul is not the end of you; it is actually the beginning of you. How would you know that God is a healer if you were never broken?

How would you know him to be the lover of your soul if you were not left alone hurting? How would you know him to be a comforter if he did not send you strength in your time of your trouble?

God desires for you to experience wholeness in him. He does not get any glory when your soul is bound, troubled, or lost.

Embrace salvation and give your soul to God. He will take great care of it.

Take advantage of the many blessings that God had for you when you became one of his own. Now that you have received salvation, receive the beauty of it.

"Affirmations are our mental vitamins, providing the supplementary positive thoughts we need to balance the barrage of negative events and thoughts we experience daily."
-Tia Walker

AFFIRMATIONS

- I Am A Child Of God!
- I Am Healed!
- I Am Delivered!
- I Am Changed!
- I Am Loved!
- I Am Forgiven!
- I Am Accepted!
- I Am Whole!
- I Am Chosen!
- I Am Protected!
- I Am Needed!
- I Am Free!
- I Am Sane!
- I Am Intelligent!
- I Am Useful!
- I Am Purposeful!
- I Am Unique!
- I Am Happy!

Shattered Greatness
"The Beauty Of Salvation"

Made in the USA
Columbia, SC
13 July 2021

41712576R00031